Chime For a Change:

How to change your behavior, attain enlightenment, transform your relationships, nurture your family, empower your friends, motivate your workplace and effect world peace using a digital watch.

By Jim Lew with Daniel Cohen

ISBN: 0-75965-144-2

This book is printed on acid free paper.

First published by Pay Attention Press
RD6 Box 6198A
Stroudsburg, PA 18360
(570) 992-6393

Printed in the United States of America

1stBooks – rev. 11/14/01

For information, please contact:
Daniel Cohen
Pay Attention Press
RR6 Box 6198A
Stroudsburg, PA 18360
(570) 992-6393

Dedication

Beep Here Now

Dedicated to Ram Dass
who helped a generation
glimpse the power
of the present.

Table of Contents

Foreword

Somewhere in our readings on the topic of mindfulness, we realized that our writing was positioned some where between the spiritual approach taken by Nobel Peace Prize nominee Thich Nhat Hanh and the academic perspective of Ellen Langer. We hope, therefore, that this book has the capacity to reach the lay reader, who may find this candid and pragmatic approach to mindfulness useful and fun. The results may nevertheless have similar effects, but, then, that's the idea. Thich Nhat Hanh, writing from a Buddhist perspective, speaks of a quality of existence that advocates a greater connectedness to the world and through it, to an "awakening" process. The seeds of this awakening lie in simple reminders integrated into one's normal life, what Thich Nhat Hanh refers to as "bells of mindfulness." Whether you seek enlightenment or simple self-improvement, we hope our suggestions help.

As to Ellen Langer's work, we can only be excited by the possibility that intentional, mindful activities can increase longevity and improve life's quality. Since much of her research is published in a domain seldom visited by most readers, we hope that this book encourages people to check out her research and read *Mindfulness* and *The Power of Mindful Learning*. It might help us improve our understanding of what it takes to live longer and better.

Acknowledgements

This book would not exist except for the help of some of my closest friends. Conceptual contributors include my late mother who introduced me to the power of persistence and repetition, my father who role-models thoughtfulness, Annie and Jack Moses, Maria Ferry, Ron and Margo Landry, Jacqui Miller, Marie Kennerson, Larrian Gillespie, Rod and Mary Gleysteen (&Josh), Joby Pritzker, Sue Crawford, Diane Stanko, Honnay Malloy, Professor Lee Lee, Max Gail, Bob Vila, Mike Ferrone, Billy Van Arsdale, Margery Nagel, Linda Ehrke, my brother Jack, and many others, who in earnest and casual conversations supported me with ideas and feedback. Sandra Oriel educated me about Thich Nhat Hanh and Gaylen Paulson turned me on to Ellen Langer.

Read this, it really is an introduction!

When I purchased my first digital watch many years ago, I notice a function called hourly chime. There were instructions in the little manual that explained how to turn it on, but no mention of what it's purpose was. I asked several people if they knew what it was for and they said no. It was then that I decided to try just mentally attaching a word to the little "beep" coming from my watch. I found the results very positive. I discovered that simply bringing a word or thought to mind up to sixteen times a day created a minor obsession with the word or concept. I found that at an unconscious level, my mind started noticing this intruder and became interested in exploring it's meaning and implications. Within a month, the intruder had become a familiar integrated function of thought and understanding. I was on my way. By the way, my first word was drawn from the book I was reading at the time, Robert Persig's ZEN AND THE ART OF MOTORCYCLE MAINTAINANCE, which was a treatise on quality.

Here is a powerful tool so simple you'll wonder that it's not already a part of your life. This idea is so simple that any individual old enough to tell time or any group, from a circle of friends to a large corporation or political organization can use it as a fulcrum with which to leverage self-prescribed change.

We all know that repetition is a key to learning and retaining new behavior. We learn the alphabet by rote. We train our dogs and attempt to train our children by repeating the same commands over and over again. New skills — in sports, knitting, juggling or video game playing — are acquired by repetition.

Even though we know the critical importance of repetition in effecting change, we don't practice it. As adults we frequently look at our lives and seek a particular enrichment, change in pattern, or shift in consciousness. Perhaps we want to remember to stand up and stretch more often during our workday, or we want to become more acknowledging of those with whom we share our lives, or we want to be more present to the wonder of the world around us. We seem to believe these changes can be accomplished by edict, resolution or choice. Mostly we do not succeed. In fact, we fail so often that many of us decide we're too weak-willed, old or rigid to make these changes. We're selling ourselves short.

We're not too weak-willed, old or rigid. We're simply not doing our homework. Just as research has demonstrated that studying how learning occurs helps us to create ways to expedite the process, learning about change can help us find more effective ways of optimizing our own development.

We're not too weak-willed, old, or rigid. What we lack is what we've always needed to acquire a new behavior pattern ... practice. We're not talking about a lot of hard work. We're talking about our own gentle, guiding hand, reminding us on a regular basis to consider our options.

How often is a regular basis? How about once an hour?

Let's say that you think you would be healthier if you stretched more often. Your back frequently gets stiff, because you sit too long. You know you should get up more often to stretch, but you don't think of it. You've tried. You've said to yourself, "Self, you should get up and stretch more often!" And it hasn't lasted very long. Maybe it lasted five days? Five hours? Five minutes?

What if once an hour you got a gentle reminder, "Psst! It's been an hour since you stretched last. How about it? Feel like getting up and taking a break?" You have the choice not to act on the thought, but at least you were reminded, and an hour from now you're going to be reminded again. In fact, at the rate of once an hour, during the 16 hours most of us are awake, you'll have 16 opportunities to practice each day. Over a week that's 112 opportunities, 480 in a month. That's enough to establish a pattern. That's enough to make a difference. No one else is involved; little or no cost is incurred. And there are so many changes that are ideal candidates for this kind of hourly reinforcement.

The technology behind this simple approach to change is a humble, digital watch. It'll chime on the hour. It'll beep in precision. It'll communicate softly, subtly that now is the time to:

- Turn to the person beside you and compliment them.
- Think of the person that you love most in the world.
- Acknowledge a coworker.
- Do ten sit-ups.

- Take a second to get grounded and become aware of where you are right this second.

It is so simple, and you can do so much with it.

How can we stretch such a simple idea into a whole book? Just wait and see. There's quite a bit of territory to explore. And while you'll be able, eventually, to add to the list, we've already spent 16 years exploring the possibilities. We're going to show you how to:

1. Work on yourself
2. Strengthen your primary relationship
3. Build self-esteem in your family
4. Develop deeper, richer relationships with your friends
5. Increase teamwork with your co-workers
6. Drive values and strategic direction within a corporation or business
7. Motivate and coordinate political action groups…

You get the idea.

A Brief History of Chime for a Change

The genesis of the ideas and tools presented here began roughly 20 years ago and were born out of having read two books. The first was Robert Persig's *Zen and the Art of Motorcycle Maintenance*. Persig's main character spoke, in an on-going conversation throughout the book, about the notion of quality. Quality. What does quality mean in our lives? What is the intrinsic quality of this moment? What am I contributing of quality to the world in which I lived? What can be done to improve the quality of a given moment? There's a lot to be learned by looking at the world through a word.

In *Island,* Aldous Huxley creates a Utopian world in which much of the success of the society was dependent upon its being fully present or mindful. One way that the society stayed present was by releasing trained birds that called out, "Attention! Attention! Here and now, boys! Here and now, boys." Although a myna, macaw or parrot is a high maintenance means of programmable reminding, the idea was most appealing. "How can we remind ourselves to pay better attention? How can we remember to be more fully present?"

Anything that shows up in your life regularly becomes a part of your understanding of the world. Regularity is the basis of all learning. Without consistency there is no learning. Consistency means that something hangs around long enough for you to figure it out. A friend of ours has created a stress reduction system based on research that indicates that it takes about 21 days before a behavior is integrated enough to become automatic. A month is a good, round figure. Stick with a new "habit" for a month and it is yours.

The late physicist, David Bohm, observed that one problem with mankind is that our thoughts are incoherent. Think about light from a regular light bulb versus light from a laser. A light bulb's photons are dispersed and incoherent. A laser's photons are focused within a narrow beam; they're made coherent (moving in the same direction), and can burn holes through metal. If you bring something to mind regularly and it is directed and focused, your thought begins to build coherence.

The Law of Occam's Razor states that the simplest, most direct explanation is usually the correct one. A corollary might be that the simplest approach is the one most easily integrated and used successfully. While many people get very excited about content, what is at least as important is method. Yes, it's a good idea to stand up and stretch, (the content) but how are you going to remember to do so (the method)? Human growth is enhanced when you master the simplest, most elegant building block: the ability to repeat, in a pleasant manner, a desired behavior until it is internalized.

The introduction of inexpensive, reliable digital watches that chime on the hour answer our needs perfectly. About twenty years ago I was conducting training programs for teachers and school administrators. Most of the programs were focused on teen drug and substance abuse and it was very difficult to do much on the subject without also talking about self-esteem and related matters. I started talking about using a digital watch as a means of reminding oneself on an hourly basis to pay attention, to think about quality, to give positive feedback, etc. Perhaps six months later I would be back at the school for a follow-up program and teachers would come up to me thanking me for having turned them on to such a simple, elegant tool. Evidently, there was some agreement for the effectiveness of this approach.

In discussing the ideas in this book with friends, they have shared two resources that we want to pass along. Thich Nhat Hanh, a Buddhist monk and Ellen Langer, a Harvard professor, have both taken up the banner of mindfulness for a large number of readers and are worth further exploration. Here are brief excerpts …

From Thich Nhat Hanh: *Bells of Mindfulness,* "In my tradition, we use the temple bells to remind us to come back to the present moment. Every time we hear the bell, we stop talking, stop our thinking and return to ourselves, breathing in and out, and smiling. Whatever we are doing, we pause for a moment and just enjoy our breathing.

"Since I have come to the West, I have not heard many Buddhist temple bells. But fortunately, there are church bells all over Europe. There do not seem to be as many in the United States; I think that is a pity. Whenever I give a lecture in Switzerland, I always make use of the church bells to practice mindfulness. When the bell rings, I stop talking, and all of us listen to the full sound of the bell. We enjoy it so much. (I think it is better than the lecture!) When we hear the bell, we can pause and enjoy our breathing and get in touch with the wonders of life that are around us — the flowers, the children, the beautiful sounds. Every time we get back in touch with ourselves, the conditions become favorable for us to encounter life in the present moment.

"One day in Berkeley, I proposed to professors and students at the University of California that every time the bell on the campus sounds, the professors and students should pause in order to breathe consciously. Everyone should take the time to enjoy being alive! We should not just be rushing around all day. We have to learn to really enjoy our church bells and our school bells. Bells are beautiful, and they can wake us up.

"If you have a bell at home, you can practice breathing and smiling with its lovely sound. But you do not have to carry a bell into your office or factory. You can use any sound to remind you to pause, breathe in and out, and enjoy the great moment …" Thich Nhat Hanh goes on to suggest that even a ringing phone or the brake lights of the car in front of you can be a bell of mindfulness.

From Ellen Langer: *Mindfulness*
Ellen J. Langer, a Harvard researcher, has studied and written extensively about the nature of mind*less*ness and mind*fuln*ess. She defines mindfulness as "a state of alertness and lively awareness" including "active information processing, characterized by cognitive differentiation: the creation of categories and distinctions. Mindfulness may be seen as creating (noticing) multiple perspectives, or being aware of context. When in this state, the person is becoming more and more differentiated while differentiating the external world." Contrast this with her definition of mindlessness, "a state of reduced attention … rigid and rule-governed rather than rule-guided." Langer states that mindlessness "involves rigidity on both cognitive and emotional levels … it is unintentional … entropy-constant." Mindfulness is characterized as "entropy-reducing," and "capacity-increasing."

She also describes the relationship of both mindlessness and mindfulness to health. In experiments where groups of elderly were observed engaged in so-called mindful activities and active meditation, results of the study indicated that compared to a less mindful group, mindfulness had a clearly observable benefit in extending life. "Three years later, no one had died in the TM (meditating) group and 87.5% of the mindful group was still alive, compared with the 62.5% of the baseline group. The mindfulness treatment also resulted in an increase in perceived control."

During the process of writing this book, others came forward to mention other champions of reminders. Gurdjieff reportedly stated that the best thing he could do for his students was to act as an alarm clock to remind them to remember to remember.

At an Internet sight called Zoofence, I read of a couple who upon awakening each day wind up a one-hour timer and when it rings they stop what they're doing and pause in thought, then reset it for the next hour. They repeat the process throughout the day and even travel with the timer.

Rupert Sheldrake's theory of morphological fields predicts that lots of people will begin to have the same thought once an idea takes root in the "morphological field" of human consciousness.

I know that some of you are way ahead at this point in the book. You've already figured out where we're going. Good. By design, this is a simple idea; you don't need to read any further, just beep it.

Chapter 1: Wrist Management

This book is about a revolution in method. The content, while powerful opportunities will be described, is strictly up to you. The method is the message. Use the hourly chime feature of a digital watch to remind yourself on a consistent basis to think (and perhaps, on occasion, to act) on a given thought.

This is DEFINITELY mind control, folks. The point is that the mind and the control are yours. If you want to avoid having your mind controlled by someone else, you'd better be ready to control it yourself.

The principle behind the method is the simplest principle of all — repetition.

Beyond method, there are two aspects worth taking seriously: content and synchronization. Regarding content, we suggest you pick a word to focus on for a month. It should be a word YOU think is worthy of being considered once an hour, as many hours as you can, for a month. The power of really coming to terms with what the word means in your life won't be apparent until the repetitions have been experienced.

Just have the word. Notice what comes up for you when the chime beeps. This method is about simplicity, just let a word circulate through your brain once an hour. Yes, you can be more active than that, but, at least initially, just let the thought of the word be enough. You can enter the Olympic chiming events later.

Let's take the word "present" for an example. Everyone can profit by becoming more present, by living more in the now. As has been said many times, many ways, the past is past and the future has yet to get here. All we really have is this moment. Yet we all tend to live anywhere but right here, right now. So many of the goodies in life are only available in the present moment and the more we remain present, the greater the access to our real lives we really have. When we live in the past, we tend to be victims of regret and when we live in the future, we tend to be victims of worry. Neither is very constructive. Being here now allows us to enjoy each breath, to feel the sun on our cheeks, to see the beauty in a tree.

So, what if, for one month, each time your watch beeps, you ask yourself to get present? Be here now! Over the course of a month you will be reminded roughly 480 times to "be here now." You'll be more attentive. You'll notice the dissolution of what gets in the way of you being more aware, more conscious, more tuned in.

Synchronization is the second aspect of working with a digital watch that can add a powerful component to your experience. What you can do on your own with your watch is quite amazing. But what you can do with a watch and other people — lovers, friends, family, and coworkers — can be VERY interesting. To capitalize on the possibilities of playing with others, synchronization becomes important. If you and your significant other have agreed that each day at work, each time you chime you will think fond thoughts of each other, it feels kind of special to know that you're doing so at exactly the same moment.

Some of you have this method pretty well figured out and now you understand more of the basic, underlying concepts. It's okay to stop reading here. Just beep it.

Chapter 2: Conquering Technophobia or My VCR Flashes 12:00

Going mano a mano with the digital timepiece

Before you can proceed to benefit from all this beeping, you must learn to master the intricacies of a digital watch. Intuition will not be a useful guide; it isn't an intuitive process. It is, however, a fairly simple one. What's between you and mastery is about 15 minutes of drill and the beliefs that (a) you can't hurt the watch and (b) that you'll succeed. By mastery, we mean that you'll be able to set the correct time and that you'll be able to turn on and off the hourly chime with aplomb.

The watch we've seen worn most often is the Timex Triathlon and we are going to describe how to tame that model in the pages that follow. Those of you using some models of Casio or Armitron watches can turn to the Appendix and see if we've included the instructions for your model there. If you don't see your watch listed, you're going to have to read the directions that came with your particular timepiece and figure it out on your own. Even if you have to buy a new digital watch, it will only set you back about $10, depending on the features you select. That is a bargain!

Let's face it, many people know about chiming watches and have negative opinions of them because of those beepers who do not turn their chimes off when they are inappropriate. Well, why don't they turn them off? Either because they do not know how or because they're insensitive to those around them. Who wants to be in church and hear a dozen unsynchronized beeps popping off across the congregation? Who wants to just be drifting off to well-earned slumber only to hear the audacity of an uncurbed beep! Who wants to be on the edge of an $8 movie seat just before the exciting conclusion, in a $25 concert seat awaiting the coda, or in a $100 theater seat in the midst of that tender love scene and hear a blasted electronic tone! There should be a law! So don't be one of these uncouth beepers. Curb your chime! Take just a few minutes to become the master of your beeps! You paid for the book; follow the directions!

(Pardon the rant, but we're in the delicate position of lobbying on the behalf of politically correct beeping and we must take our subject material seriously. Please, be a considerate beeper.)

It's so simple. We're going to go through this as a drill. Having already sung the praises of repetition, we're going to model the practice in this instruction process. First, in the interests of synchronization, you're going to go through a six-step process for setting the time on your watch. We'll repeat the process five times. Then, we'll learn to turn the chime on and off. That will be a three-step process. We'll repeat that procedure several times. At the conclusion, you may feel wrung dry by effort, but the satisfaction of a sweat well-earned will be fair compensation for the exertion. Not only that, but all those around you will appreciate the effort as well.

Setting the time

Many people have taken digital readouts to task. There are eloquent arguments about the merits of analog versus digital timepieces. The arguments go something like, "Who really wants to know if it is 5:31 as opposed to 5:30? How precise do we need to be?" Well, we're going to show you several reasons why this precision can be very valuable and useful. We want you to be very precise about this one thing. But, we're not going to talk about it now; we're going to do that later. We're just building the case for why we want you to make a phone call to a 900 number. You see, 900-410-TIME is the number for the National Observatory. You may recall having heard in grade school that this is THE clock for the whole world. This is as close to absolute time as the planet has been able to agree upon. All you have to do to keep the same time as everyone else who's read this book and is aspiring to the same goals as you is to call that number and follow the following directions. But before we ask you to spend 50¢ on a 900 number, we're gonna drill!

Look at the following diagram (because, if you're like many of us, you'll need a magnifying glass to read the watch face itself).

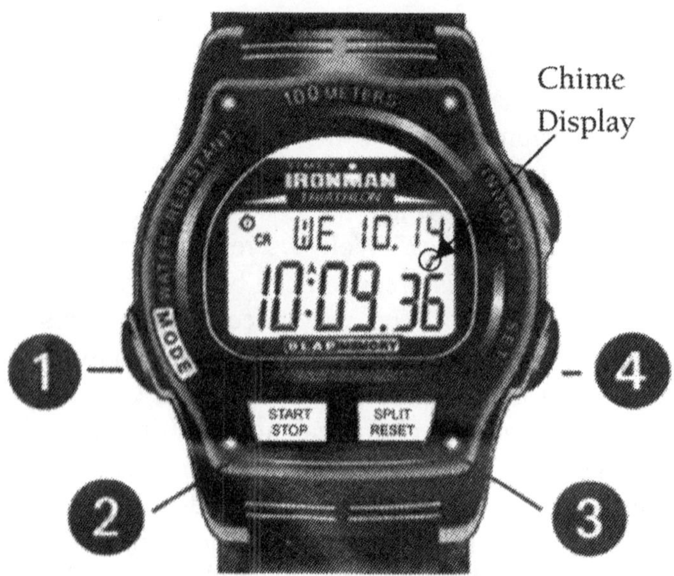

The watch has five buttons. You're only going to use four of them. Just to keep this simple, we'll call them 1, 2, 3 and four. We'll start by setting your watch for noon on Thursday, January 1 — New Years Day.

1. Press Button #4 until the word "HOLD" appears and then disappears and you notice the seconds are flashing. That takes about two seconds.

2. Press Button #3 once and the seconds go to "00".

3. Press button #2 to set the hours flashing. Press button #3 to advance the hour once per press, or hold it down to set the hours streaming.

4. Press button #2 again to flash the minutes. Press button #3 to advance the minutes.

5. Press button #2 again to advance month, then date and then day of week. And press button #3 to advance each in turn.

6. Press button #4 to end the setting process.

That wasn't so hard. Let's repeat that process. Start with step #1 and set your watch for Christmas morning — 6:00 AM on Sunday, December 25.

1. Press Button #4 until the seconds flash.

2. Press Button #3 to zero out the seconds.

3. Press button #2 to set the hours flashing. Press button #3 to advance the hour.

4. Press button #2 again to flash the minutes. Press button #3 to advance them.

5. Press button #2 again to advance month, then date and then day of week. And press button #3 to advance each in turn.

6. Press button #4 to end the setting process.

Fantastic! Now, set your watch for the fireworks — 9:00 PM on Sunday, July 4.

1. Press Button #4 until the seconds flash.

2.   Press Button #3 to zero out the seconds.

3.   Press button #2 to set the hours flashing. Press button #3 to advance the hour.

4.   Press button #2 again to flash the minutes. Press button #3 to advance them.

5.   Press button #2 again to advance month, then date and then day of week. And press button #3 to advance each in turn.

6.   Press button #4 to end the setting process.

One more drill and we'll dial the 900 number. Set your watch for Day Light Savings Time — 2:00 AM on Saturday, April 15.

1.   Press Button #4 until the seconds flash.

2.   Press Button #3 to zero out the seconds.

3.   Press button #2 to set the hours flashing. Press button #3 to advance the hour.

4.   Press button #2 again to flash the minutes. Press button #3 to advance them.

5.   Press button #2 again to advance month, then date and then day of week. And press button #3 to advance each in turn.

6.   Press button #4 to end the setting process.

All right! Now, get ready. This call will cost 50¢. When you dial 900-410-TIME, you'll hear a man reading the time in 5- and 10- second intervals. (What a boring job.) He'll say something like, "US Naval Observatory Master Clock. At the tone Eastern Daylight Time 16 hours, 45 minutes and 50 seconds. US Naval Observatory Master Clock. At the tone Eastern Daylight Time 16 hours, 45 minutes and 55 seconds." Remember, your watch's seconds zero out when you press button #3, so you will be waiting like a puma ready to pounce, when this joker says, "US Naval Observatory Master Clock. At the tone Eastern Daylight Time 16 hours, 46 minutes exactly." So, get your watch ready; cradle the phone and dial 900-410-TIME.

1. Press Button #4 until the seconds flash.

2. Press Button #3 to zero out the seconds when he says the word "exactly."

3. Press button #2 to set the hours flashing. Press button #3 to advance the hour. Remember that he is reading the time for Eastern Daylight time; you will need to take this into consideration.

4. Press button #2 again to flash the minutes. Press button #3 to advance them.

5. Press button #2 again to advance month, then date and then day of week. And, of course, press button #3 to advance each in turn. The guy from the observatory won't help with these items.

6. Press button #4 to end the setting process.

Congratulations! You can now travel from time zone to time zone, fall back in the Fall and spring forward in the Spring. And you're precisely synchronized. All that remains is the matter of learning to turn the chime off and on. This is so easy!

Chime On, Chime Off

To set the chime on and off you only need to use buttons #1 and #3. Check out the diagram. See the little circle? That is where the little symbol for the chime will appear. If you look at your watch and see nothing, that is because the chime is not turned on. Here's how it works:

1. Press button #1 three times. You'll notice the word "ALARM" fill the screen.

2. Press button #3 once. Then again. Then again. Then again. You'll notice the watch cycles through displaying that little mark.

3. Press button #3 again to end the process.

So, let's try this. Press button #1 three times to bring up the "ALARM" screen. Press button #3 until you are sure the chime is turned off. Press Button #1 once to end the process. You've just turned off the chime and are ready for church, bed or the cinema.

You awake in the morning. You're ready to begin your day's beeping. You grab your watch (come on, let's do this, now) press button #1 three times, press button #3 once or until you see that little mark, press button #1 once.

Time to go to the movies? Press button #1 three times, Button #3 once, and button #1 once. That's it, dude. Done. You're trained. Ready to take your place in responsible beeping society. I'm proud of you. Your pew-sitting neighbors are proud of you and admit it, you're proud of yourself. Right?

Chapter 3: Beep All that You Can Beep

There are many incredible advantages to beeping in the plural and we'll address those perks in subsequent chapters. But since this is a book about simplicity and change, we begin with the simplest configuration: the single beeper.

As we discussed in the Introduction and Chapter 1: Wrist Management, a chiming watch can be a formidable agent of change. Through the basic principle of repetition, it's easy to slowly, gently and elegantly effect change in ourselves. If we reflect for a moment and consider what we could do that would have the greatest impact on the quality of our lives, for many of us the list would have greatly overlapping elements. Almost all of us would agree that becoming more present, more attentive, more "here and now" would be a significant step forward. Most of us would agree that becoming more aware of the quality we experience and create in our lives would likewise be valuable. Being more conscious of our listening; becoming more attuned to our intention; acknowledging others more often; appreciating the world around us; experimenting with kindness (which the Dalai Lama refers to as the greatest good) are sort of like Mom, the flag and apple pie — how do you argue with them?

We've selected some words (a baker's dozen) for your consideration. For each word we've included dictionary definitions and a few notes which may be of assistance in your thinking. You could do worse than to spend a month with each of these words. In other words, for one month, each time your watch chimes let yourself think for a moment about one particular word. This selection represents a full year of suggestions. Don't, however, feel bound by this selection. We've also included a list of additional worthy words. Please feel free to draw up your own lists as well. Don't feel compelled to spend a month on each. It could be more than a month. I beeped on the word "transparency," for a year and a half. It could be less than a month. Sometimes a word that elicits an immediate negative reaction is exactly the *right* word from which you can or should learn. Remember that it's your mind, your control. You pick the word.

There is, of course, no right experience of these words. We've attempted to select words that have constructive, positive meanings, but your experience may not always be lofty. For instance, in considering the word "listening," you may become aware that you don't feel listened to in some aspect of your life. The quality of that experience may not feel great, but you'll probably find that there is learning associated with the experience.

If you wish to reinforce the impact of the repeated word, consider ripping the page from the book, writing the word on a 5" X 7" index card or Post-It™ note and sticking it on your refrigerator, bathroom mirror, file cabinet, dashboard — anywhere you're likely to let your eyes frequently focus. Or, when you hear the beep, write the word down on a piece of paper, repeat it under your breath, shout it out loud. You can do anything that will provide you with an opportunity to really consider the concept at hand.

If you notice that you stop hearing the chime or hear it only on rare occasions, don't worry. But do take a look at Chapter 6: Troubleshooting.

The Ecology of Change

What happens when things really start changing? How will it affect those around you and how will you handle being different? In therapy these are called secondary gain considerations. Most of us have managed to get some mileage (read attention) from our problems. What happens if you solve those problems? It isn't quite as simple as it may seem. Take some time and imagine all of the unplanned effects of any particular change you might make in your life. No more complaining or suffering out loud. What will you do with your time? Could being more of a winner feel strange? You bet. If it's new, it'll feel strange.

So, without further ado, we welcome you to a full year of beeps, a brave new world, the world of your mind and your control.

Attention:

[L attention-, attentio, fr. attendere]
- Concentration of the mental powers upon an object; a close or careful observing or listening.
- The ability or power to concentrate mentally.
- Observant consideration; notice: *Your suggestion has come to our attention.*
- Consideration or courtesy: *attention to others' feelings.*

Attention is about realizing what is so in your world right this second. It is about bringing your consciousness into this particular "now." In this instant, what is happening? In this instant, how do you feel? What do you see? Smell? Hear? Know? It is the moment the hypnotist snaps his fingers, we come out of the trance and wake fully into our lives. By the way, if you need permission to snap out of your life trance, you certainly have ours. You might recall the film, *MATRIX*, which metaphorically speaks to how much of "reality" is supplied to us by powerful interests.

Try this word as your default for any beep moments when you don't have a particular word you're working with or can't quite recall one.

Quality:

[L qualitat-, qualitas, fr. qualis of what kind]
1. a. An inherent or distinguishing characteristic; a property.
2. b. A personal trait, especially a character trait: *someone with few redeeming qualities.*
3. Essential character; nature: *Mahogany has the quality of being durable.*
4. a. Superiority of kind: *an intellect of unquestioned quality.*
5. b. Degree or grade of excellence: *yard goods of low quality.*

While none of these words are "easy," perhaps "quality" leads the pack in terms of the quantity of serious philosophy written. Don't let that intimidate you. What does the word mean for you? What is the quality of this moment? This day? What quality have you added to your experience? Once you begin to become conscious of the quality of the moment, ask yourself, "How do I feel about this?" If you like it, great. If you don't, what are your options?

Intention:

[L intentia, intentian-, fr. intentus, intent, from past participle of intendere, to direct attention.]

1. A course of action that one intends to follow.
2. An aim that guides action; an objective.
3. Purpose with respect to marriage: *honorable intentions.*
4. Philosophy. A concept arising from directing the attention toward an object.

Are you conscious of your intention? Can you state, at any given moment, what you want to have happen? What is your desired outcome? Are you direct? Do your desired outcomes get shaped as positives or negatives? Are you choosing something you want or working to avoid something? Are you more motivated by desire or fear? How committed are you to your intention? Is there a gap between your intention and your outcome?

Creativity

From Create [from Latin creEre, to bring forth, create, produce "to cause to grow"]

1. Having the power or ability to create things.
2. Showing imagination and originality as well as routine skill, creative work.
3. One who displays productive originality.

That you have gotten this far in this book is your certification of creativity: you saw the possibilities. Your life is your canvas and your mind is the medium. Let it rip! Solve problems. Evoke beauty. Add the finishing touch to a meal, a report, a letter, a thought, a compliment. It may seem obvious, but one must create to develop creativity. Create something daily. You probably do anyway, it's time you notice and give yourself credit.

Compassion:

[L com- + pati to bear with, suffer with.]

1. Sympathetic consciousness of others' distress together with a desire to alleviate it.

Compassion is the force of understanding that can bridge our differences. Compassion implies understanding and a reaching supportiveness. Compassion begs an action.

You might ask yourself:

- Who around me is suffering?
- What might they be feeling?
- Is there an appropriate response that I want to take in the face of their distress?

What would happen if you did this once an hour?

Acknowledge:

[Probably blend of Middle English knowlechen, to acknowledge (from knowen, to know) and Middle English aknouen, to recognize.]

1. a. To admit the existence, reality or truth of.
2. b. To recognize as being valid or having force or power.
3. a. To express recognition of: *acknowledge a friend's smile.*
4. b. To express thanks or gratitude for.
5. To report the receipt of.
6. Law: To accept or certify as legally binding: *acknowledge a deed.*

It is amazing how we can walk through a crowd on the street, wait in a line, walk to the water cooler at the office and acknowledge no one.

How do humans acknowledge each other? We can look squarely at one another. We can greet each other. We can touch. We can tell each other that we matter in the world. Work with this word for a month and you'll have roughly 480 opportunities to let those around you know that you know that they exist, that they have rights, that they make a difference. Can you imagine the impact it would make if everyone did this? For children? For couples? For subordinates? For employers?

Gratefulness:

[From obsolete grate, pleasing, from Latin grEtus.]

1. Appreciative of benefits received; thankful.
2. Expressing gratitude.
3. Affording pleasure or comfort; agreeable.

We are at the banquet table of life. We've been seated here so long, that we fail, in most circumstances, to be aware of it. We are like a fish in water that is unaware it is in water.

Check in once an hour. How are you blessed? What's going well? Who do you have to thank? What does it cost to express gratitude?

Saying "Thank you," 16 times a day reframes your experience of the world in which you live, shifting your attention from what's missing to what's in abundance. It lifts you to a place of increased awareness of the opportunities, the surplus and the sufficiency that surround you. Let's hear it for the grateful beep!

Relationship:

[L. relEtus, past participle of referre : re-, re- + lEtus, brought again.]

1. The condition or fact of being related; connection or association.
2. Connection by blood or marriage; kinship.
3. A particular type of connection existing between people related to or having dealings with each other: *has a close relationship with his siblings.*
4. A romantic or sexual involvement.

Our greatest joys and our greatest pains are frequently associated with our relationships.

With whom are you relating right now? Yourself? Your partner? Your children? Your co-workers? Clients? What is the quality of that connection? How are you exercising your creativity, your passion, your caring and your intention in regard to that relationship? What or who is included in your awareness of relationship? Do you relate to the person pouring your coffee? In the film *Castaway*, Tom Hanks retains his sanity by forming a relationship with a volleyball.

Listening:

[ME listnen, fr. OE hlysnan, OE hlud loud] vt archaic: to give ear to: hear]

1. To pay attention to sound.
1. To hear something with thoughtful attention; give consideration.
2. To be alert to catch an expected sound.

Give yourself a grade for the past hour: How well did you pay attention to sound? How well did you hear with thoughtful attention, with consideration? Were you alert? If you listened well, what difference has it made? If you did not listen well, has that made a difference to those around you? What would it take to become more skilled (besides a reminder each hour)? Are you more aware of the listening of others? What comes up for you observing how others listen?

Kindness

from Kind [Middle English, natural, kind, from Old English gecynde, natural.]

1. The quality or state of being kind.
2. An instance of kind behavior: *I will always remember your many kindnesses to me.*

According to the Dalai Lama, kindness is the greatest good.

A good friend bought a vanity license plate with the word "kindness" and reports that it has contributed both to the quality of his driving and to the reactions he draws from others on the road. Ever heard anyone say that a person was too kind and really mean it?

Being kind is not inherently difficult; it requires thoughtfulness, awareness and intention. It requires remembering. Beep.

Power

[L. potis, able, powerful.]

1. The ability or capacity to perform or act effectively.
2. A specific capacity, faculty or aptitude: *her powers of concentration.*
3. Strength or force exerted or capable of being exerted; might.
4. The ability or official capacity to exercise control; authority.
5. A person, group or nation having great influence or control over others.
10. Physics: The rate at which work is done, expressed as the amount of work per unit time and commonly measured in units such as the watt and horsepower.

Some of us hide out. We pretend not to have the capacity to perform or act effectively. Do you acknowledge your power? Where is the power in your life? Does the exercise of power in your life look more like a continuous battle or more like the way water courses around rock? To many of us, the word "power" has a negative connotation. Why?

Integrity

[L. integritEs, soundness, from integer, whole, complete.]

1. Steadfast adherence to a strict moral or ethical code.
2. The state of being unimpaired; soundness.
3. The quality or condition of being whole or undivided; completeness.

Integrity is about being able to look at ourselves in the mirror of our consciousness. Are we able to consider our behavior and find it reasonably consistent with our beliefs? The degree to which we vary from our beliefs of right action is the degree to which we're not whole, impaired and unsound. What do you believe? Are you of your word? What is between you and you?

Complete

[Middle English complet, from Latin completus, past participle of complere, to fill out.]

1. To bring to a finish or an end: *She has completed her studies.*
2. To make whole, with all necessary elements or parts: *A second child would complete their family.*

Before you can add wine to a full glass you must empty it. Sometimes our lives are so full of incomplete enterprises that we cannot really tell how we're doing. At such times beginning a new project is lunacy, a prescription for failure. Even maintaining all that we have in some stage of progress may be out of the question. Sometimes completing means doing a lot of work. Sometimes it is a matter of doing the last step. Sometimes it means that even though you haven't arrived at your originally planned outcome, that you are changing your plan, you're not going to get to that particular outcome. And you do that by just asserting that you're finished, done, complete.

Other Worthy Words

The previous 12 words are very powerful words. Few of us will fail to grow if we really apply ourselves to considering each for a month. Those seeking still more grist for the mill might ponder these worthy words.

Ability
Abundance
Adaptiveness
Appreciation
Ardor
Assertiveness
Authenticity
Authority
Awareness
Balance
Beauty
Begin
Breathe
Blessing
Care
Charity
Charm
Child-likeness
Civility
Coherence
Communicate
Competence
Concentration
Congruity

Conscious
Courtesy
Design
Desired Outcome
Destiny
Dynamism
Empathy
Encourage
Energy
Enhance
Enlightenment
Enthusiasm
Excitement
Facility
Faith
Feeling
Fidelity
Flow
Focus
Forgiveness
Fortitude
Fortune
Freedom
Friendship
Generosity
Goodness
Grace
Harmony
Health
Honor
Humility
Humor
Inclusion

Intelligence
Intensity
Judgment
Laughter
Light
Love
Luck
Maintain
Meaning
Nourish
Observation
Openness
Passion
Peace
Play
Pleasure
Poise
Politeness
Possibility
Potential
Prosperity
Purpose
Reflection
Regard
Reliability
Respect
Responsibility
Serenity
Skill
Smell
Strength
Stretch
Tact

Thoughtfulness
Touch
Truth
Veracity
Thankfulness
Vessel
Vigor
Virtue
Warmth
Will
Wisdom
Work
Zeal

Other Ways to Use Your Watch

Certain mental practices become "gates" to different levels of mind activity. These different levels, research seems to imply, are also part of whole body responses. Changing or altering consciousness is often accompanied by systemic changes such as lowered heart rates, lowered blood pressure and changes in blood chemistry.

Each of us can develop behaviors and activities that change the quality of our thoughts and mental processes in predictable ways. For instance, some people, when they want to generate new ideas, go for a drive and carry a handheld tape recorder. Motion seems to trigger a periodic cascade of images and conceptual ideas. Others report similar responses in the shower or while listening to certain musical pieces.

One of the ways we can alter our consciousness is by simply changing our current mental activity by deciding to focus on a new imagination process. For instance, I love flying. I fly sailplanes, ultralight aircraft and gyroplanes. When I start to fantasize about flying, I get a big grin on my face and disappear into a state of very pleasurable mental daydreaming. I'm sure that changes must be happening at all levels of my body chemistry as I relax into internal images of treetop-level flying. I come out of these reveries feeling relaxed, enthusiastic and satisfied. Thinking about old friends and past loves can also greatly affect my present emotional state.

Any of these "gateway" emotional activities can be triggered by a watch beep. Make an inventory of your favorite mental activities to be your gateway list. Recently I was on the road for several weeks and suffering physically from several painful conditions. I comforted myself by thinking of caring friends when my watch beeped.

One of the yardsticks of psychological maturity is the ability to "self-comfort." (David Schnarch, *Passionate Marriage*, W.W. Norton, 1997.) It's a marker for what behavioral theorists term "individuation." We must all contend with the "intrapersonal relationship." How do we treat ourselves? What is the quality of our internal "self-talk?" Like much else in life, our self-talk is better intentional than accidental. When we choose the conversations we have with ourselves, they're generally more positive than the thoughts of an undisciplined mind. One can start with some of the recommended mental forays described in Robert Masters and Jean Houston's *Mind Games*. There are many other books that contain guides to the power of intentional mental imagery.

Carol and Carl Simonton's work demonstrates the power periodic, chosen internal imagery can have to positively affect cancer treatment outcomes. Their work, described in the books *The Healing Journey* and *Getting Well Again*, articulates how patients can be assisted in choosing powerful images that help in their healing power. As with so many such processes, a key to long-term success is in repetition, in remembering that it is time to once again bring "that" thought forward. By taking a simple methodology and matching it with some powerful linguistic ammunition, a self-help program can be self-designed, self-administered and self-evaluated. You've probably got a good four years of work represented in just this chapter. Congratulate yourself on a very economical book purchase. You did well!

But wait! There's more …

Chapter 4: Synchronicity and Synergy

With Every Beep of My Heart:Beeping in Pairs

Let's say that your relationship isn't working as beautifully as it could. Perhaps, like many other people, you know that you're much more interested in the beginnings of something, particularly a relationship. Unless you take specific action, you'll become less and less attentive to your partner.

What if every time you beep you tell your partner something you really appreciate about them. "You know Annie, I just love the way you laugh." "When you smile at me across a room, I'm just tickled I'm with you. How did I get so lucky?"

Or, you can choose to get physical. You can choose to reach out and touch your partner. Kiss. Hug. Rub shoulders. Give some physical expression of your affection.

Your partner may get suspicious. He or she might say, "You know, every time your watch beeps, you seem to be kissing or rubbing me. What's going on?" Tell the truth! Dare to be transparent. Say, "You know, I didn't think I was paying enough attention to you and thought that if I reminded myself to let you know that I feel affectionate toward you that that would be a good thing. What do you think? Are you up to being more frequently kissed, stroked, hugged and generally adored?" Don't expect to encounter much resistance. In fact, your partner will probably end up chiding you if you miss a beep that they hear!

What if when the chime goes off you're not around your significant other? Try just thinking about this person: what do you value, cherish or admire about them. You may even choose to share some of those thoughts later. "You know, my watch beeped at 1:00 this afternoon and I was reminded about how you stood up for me the other day with your mom and it just brought a grin to my face. Thank you for your loyalty. I really appreciate how much you love me."

This is a very powerful thing to do. In fact, it's miraculous. It transforms both your partner's and your own experience of the relationship. It is really quite simple and obvious. Saying something or doing something makes more of a difference than not saying or doing something.

So often when we're with people, people we like, people we have chosen to be with, we actually allow ourselves to be distanced from them. The watch becomes a reminder to get present, to reach out, to communicate and express affection.

This works well when one party in the relationship is playing. Imagine that both of you are playing! Imagine both of you synchronizing your watches so that you beep at precisely the same moment? Every time your watches beep and you're together, you can both reach out to each other. You can both be reminded to value, cherish, express your affections in some demonstrative, affectionate manner. Things could get very interesting. And if you aren't together? Every time your chime sounds, you know that someone very dear to you is thinking of you — and in a very flattering way — at that precise moment. Powerful medicine.

Another way to use the chime in relationship is in trying to better understand the other person's position. Let's say you're having a disagreement about how you spend your free time. The strategies you typically employ have not been effective and the two of you decide that another approach is needed. You could agree that when you chime, you will take a moment to try to see the other person's point of view, to try to get a new insight, or to get improved clarity. You agree to try this for a couple days, or perhaps even a week and then to try working it out again. The beep becomes a referential index.

So, you made a modest investment in buying this peculiar little book and so far, without having to work too hard, you've learned to seek personal enlightenment and to transform the quality of your relationship. But you haven't finished reading the book. There must be more!

Sly and the Family Beep: The Power of Synergy

It was pointed out in the last chapter that you can make a huge difference in interpersonal dynamics in just a couple seconds per hour. You can do it when you're with the people you love and you can even do it when you're apart from them. You have the capability of making a significant difference acting alone. You don't even have to tell people what you're doing; it can be your secret. Or you can be completely open about it.

But the impact is disproportionately multiplied through the power of synergy. Synergy can be described in the terms of a study in which newly graduated law students, setting up in solo practices for themselves, made "X" dollars of compensation in their first year. Two such newly graduated students, however, going into practice together, made five times that amount in their first year. One plus one equals five.

In the same vein, beeping in alignment with others is more powerful in effecting change — and in having fun, in fostering community, in making a difference — than is beeping alone.

The Paternal Beeper

The family unit offers many opportunities for synergistic beeping. How about once an hour catching someone doing something right? Ken Blanchard, author of *The One Minute Manager* and *The One Minute Parent* writes eloquently about the value of catching subordinates and children doing something right versus catching them doing something wrong. It is a wonderful concept and a wonderful strategy for reinforcing the behaviors you chose in others.

The chief difficulty in this enterprise lies in remembering to do the catching. Don't we have a mechanism for just this kind of reinforcement? Once an hour is not a bad interval.

Nor is this strategy limited to parent-toward-child interactions. "Dad, I love it when you spend some time with me," is a great statement for encouraging parental interaction. "Honey, I really appreciated that you ran interference with the kids while I got my running in. Thank you."

Get everyone a watch. At $10 apiece, it's a very small investment in making the family a more positively attuned environment in which you all can grow.

Families can also use beeps as a way to manage time. Kids can watch TV until the next beep. Maybe chores should be done by the beep. Find someone to hug on the beep. Or compliment. Or thank. What needs reinforcing in your family? Affection? Appreciation? Timeliness? Respect? Fun? Communication? Doing them all by turn is an option. But simply working together — figuring out what to work on, catching each other doing well, enjoying the laughter that will come to accompany the beeping — will make the modest investment so worthwhile. Don't miss this opportunity to play as a family, it's too good to pass up.

I Get by with a Little Beep from My Friends

In spite of really wanting to write this book, because of the busyness of my life, I was getting nowhere. I wanted to complete it, but needed to clear my decks and get some help. Here's what we did …

Three friends (who hadn't previously met) and I boarded a houseboat on Lake Powell for a week. I timeshare this houseboat twice a year and had been trying to get these people to come join me for a trip for a long time. All three of them knew that in addition to taking in the beauty of the desert in full spring bloom, that we'd also be working on this book.

Before boarding we bought 4 identical watches at a discount store for roughly $10 each. The first morning we strapped brand new, fully-synchronized digital watches to our wrists. We also wrote out a set of roughly 25 slips of paper that each contained a single word and threw them in a bucket. The words were chosen in a collaborative brainstorming session of roughly 15 minutes and included: attention, faith, taste, intention, adventure, stretch, magic, generosity, quality, humor, touch, encouragement, etc., words just like those in Chaprter 3. Each morning we each drew a word and shared that word with the others. As the day progressed, each beep brought a giggle followed by a recitation of the drawn words. "Humor?" "Stretch!" "Faith!" "Taste." With each passing hour, we'd reflected on our individual word and would then share our thoughts with the group.

The process had several interesting results. First, there was the individual effect of working on our chosen word. For one of our party, the word "Faith" came up two days in a row and was particularly appropriate for her circumstances. A day after boarding the houseboat, she received news of a major crisis that appeared to threaten both her business and several close relationships. In some ways, it would have been easy to have left the trip, or to have spent the trip in a state of upset. Working on "Faith" and being supported by the rest of us, she was able to let go of the worry, be present, enjoy herself and know that things would work out. They did.

Second, the group benefited from all the individual work. One person having "Encouragement" made for a regular infusion of positive feedback to the rest of us. Another person working on "Taste" was encouraged to cook. "Humor" was shared and "Touch" led to shoulder rubs.

Another perk was the excitement, enthusiasm and sense of community that was built from the event of each beep. It became a sort of race to shout first when you heard your chime go off. This was followed by giggling, reporting insights, getting reminded about which word each was studying. As we split up to hike, swim, meditate, read, quilt, cook, etc. hearing a beep meant that you instantly thought of where everyone else was. And it meant that we also knew each of us was in the thoughts of the rest of the group.

There is no question that a bond was formed between the four of us because of what the simple repetitive beep came to mean to the group. The four of us lead very busy lives that don't interface all that often. But the bonds that were forged on that trip, largely out of the experience of sharing the beeps, will last a very long time for us all.

Is there a chance you might not be able to get your friends to go along with a scheme like this? Sure, they might think it a preposterous thing to do. But then, if you don't make the possibility available, you'll never have the opportunity for an incredibly fun way to connect with a small group of people.

A quick review… Individual self-improvement? Check. A means to transform your primary relationship? Yep. A way to build affection and positive relationships in the family? Right on! And now a way to have a great time with your buds? Sure thing! This beeping is better than a Swiss Army knife! And wait, there's more…

Beeping While You Work

I often think I'd do better in corporate consulting if I just left a selection of words and some watches. So much corporate training is really brilliant, but individual programs frequently lack the consistency and follow-through that would make them truly successful.

Using a watch chime is not a particularly brilliant or complex strategy. It is, however, an absolutely simple and powerful way to bring a thought, value, mission or objective to mind and to integrate it, weaving it into the lives of a work group of any size.

All success is based upon control of the mind. Mind control has a negative connotation about it, but the fact of the matter is that people who have no control go nowhere. People who have brilliant control over their minds are able to direct their thoughts. They remember to think about the things that are important and follow them through to a logical conclusion.

Here are a couple ideas about how to use chiming in a work group:

- Vis-à-vis Deming: A group of customer service representatives might be asked how they're going *beyond* their customers' expectations. After an introductory meeting, their assignment is that once an hour they will ask themselves, "Do my customers have any doubt that I was really trying to serve them?"

- Groups don't need to be reminded of things they do already. If a group gathers for coffee, they don't need a chime for that. Resistance does develop, however, around change, around new behavior. How much resistance you think you can overcome is a critical judgment call. For instance, you probably wouldn't want to try to get a group of conservative males to consider their thoughts and feeling about homophobia every time their watch chimed. It would be too big a leap. They might, however, be asked to think about the consequences of unwanted physical contact versus acceptable expressions of friendship, emotional expression, assertiveness, giving feedback or owning your own experience. Those might work better with such a group.

Beeping in Movements

Ah, the power of synchronization… I'm reminded of Arlo Gutherie's *Alice's Restaurant* here. "Imagine 500 people walkin' in, singin' a bar of *Alice's Restaurant* in four-part harmony, with full orchestration and walking out. They'd think it was a movement. And friends, that's what it is …"

The implications of using a watch to facilitate the work of a group are quite exciting and the possibilities are as vast as our imaginations.

A friend uses synchronized digital watches to work with a prayer group. The group believes in the healing power of prayer and in their biweekly meetings they agree who and what it is for which they will pray. The chime provides an almost perfect means of assuring the coordination of their efforts.

Certainly more traditional methods of grassroots organizing can also benefit from this method. If a large environmental group decided to encourage all 300,000 of their members to call their senators on the stroke of 2:00, it might overload computerized switchboards all over Washington. Electronic bulletin board systems may be vulnerable. I wonder about radio talk shows? The list goes on.

Association or PAC newsletters could carry weekly or monthly instructions to their readers or members regarding what to associate with their hourly beeps. Alternately, groups could set up 800 or 900 number telephone lines to communicate to members what the current "beep to action" should be.

Of course, the key to these opportunities is synchronization. The (900) 410-TIME number provides an ideal means of assuring that everyone is in step.

Now here is the "Conspiracy Theory" angle on this: How do you keep your group's identity distinct from the group down the hall? It wouldn't do to have Operation Rescue on the same chime as NOW or the NRA on the same wavelength as the anti-NRA forces. The answer? You could synchronize on the 10th second after the proper time. You could go anywhere and have a pretty good idea of whose company you were in based on the beeps around you. Then you'd only have to worry about infiltrators!

Or you could combine the beep with a gesture. Perhaps touching the center of your chest with the fingertips of your right hand, on the beep, would be a signal recognized by your fraternity. Hmm… sounds like Spy vs. Spy!

The Heartbeep of the Planet

So what might become of all this beeping? What is the most powerful extreme to which we could aspire?

Our wildest dream … the entire world adopting the custom of pausing on the hour—every hour—to confer a moment of consideration to those around us. One thing that happens at exactly the same moment around the globe is the minute hand reaching 12 (digital :00). Imagine a significant portion (the transcendental meditation people say 10% is enough) of the world pausing at exactly the same moment to create a moment of positive attitude. Look around to see who's joining you. Cynics might see it as behavioral smiley face. I dream a world transformed.

People, on a global basis, would become accustomed to checking into their intentions and impact more frequently (they're often not the same.) Pilots know that checking their location and heading frequently get them to the right place at the right time. What if being attentive caught on at the world level? People would discover that growing, learning, and changing does not have to be so difficult and painful. Indeed, it can be as easy as associating a thought with a sound. Imagine that.

Chapter 5: Beeping for Overachievers

There's at least one in every group. You can show folks how to almost effortlessly change their lives, make love last, kindle the familial flames, have more fun with their friends, work more effectively, start the revolution and they're still not satisfied.

Some people want to work harder. In most instances, we think they should use the watch to slow down. Get a grip. Chill out. But, if you're going to insist, here are some ideas for the truly driven.

Going Beyond Having the Word

There's no rule that says you can't do more than consider an idea. For instance, take the word "stretch." Once an hour you could actually get up and stretch. It could significantly reduce your chiropractic bill. You could choose to do stomach crunches on the hour. One more each hour than the hour before? You could clean something on each beep. Or you could finish something.

90-Minute Beeping

The great hypnotherapist, Milton Erickson, believed that we have a 90-minute cycle of suggestibility. In other words, once in every 90 minutes, there's a time that you're more suggestible and 90 minutes later you'll be at the suggestible end of another cycle. Clearly, if Milton was correct, it would be better to beep in time with your 90-minute cycle. But, alas, your watch only beeps on the 60-minute hour. Setting the alarm to go off every 90 minutes is too much work for even the most challenged overachiever. What's the answer? Some of the Timex Indiglo Iron Man models have an interval timer. The watch costs about fifty dollars but will absolutely get the job done—provided you can establish when you're at your most suggestible. Try starting at what you consider a "peak moment."

Short Interval Beeping

Short interval beeping is often useful for breaking bad habits or intensive change efforts. Changing posture, for example, can be a very difficult habit to break and requires frequent self-reminders. Setting the same watch as described above in "90-Minute Beeping" to a 15-minute cycle should provide enough reinforcement to do the trick. There are also several shareware computer timers that can be set for any given interval.

Anchoring for Extra Power

Neuro Linguistic Programming (NLP) talks about anchoring. Anchoring is based on the simple principle that any two things that happen together are recorded in our brains as connected and the events tend to stay connected. If you were to press on your shoulder on a given particular point while feeling a certain emotion, you will actually start to experience that same emotion if you later pressed on the same spot again. You would have "anchored" that positive feeling to that place on your body.

In real life, unconscious anchoring works like this. Someone in your family wears a certain expression on their face every time they yell at you. Later, you get scared every time you recognize a similar expression on anyone's face. Kids often connect the doctor's offices with shots and start crying as soon as they arrive in the waiting room. You probably get a smile on your face when you answer the phone and hear an old friend's voice.

NLP teaches us to use anchoring to our advantage by deliberately arranging for two things to happen together. You could anchor strong positive feelings with a finger pressing on a shoulder, wrist or knee. Then, you can replay that positive feeling later when feeling scared. The scary feelings would then get all mixed up with the good feelings and the power of the fear would disappear. The technique is routinely used to cure phobias in minutes.

You can also use sounds as anchors. One of the reasons the beep of your watch can truly transform your life is that it becomes an anchor for whatever you choose to match to it. In our use, we've attached so many positive words and phrases to our beeps that they not only conjure up our latest interest, it also brings up the powerfully positive emotions associated with many of the life-changing visions and ideas we've already experienced from this work. There's a cumulative bonus. It becomes a tonic of vitality every hour. A beep may not be the ultimate anchor, but it sure is a persistent one.

Learn to anchor your own chosen thoughts to the beep and deepen your investigation of where your own ideas might lead you. Inevitably friends will ask what you're thinking when your watch beeps. This creates opportunities to bring up some of your latest thoughts to discuss with them. In reality, most people are ready and willing to engage with someone that tries to add a little depth to a conversation. If you believe in practicing the skilled transparency addressed by Brad Blanton in his book *Radical Honesty*, beeping opens the door for that process to take place regularly.

Random Reminders

We just heard about a small electronic device worn around the neck. Randomly, within a time frame of between two and nine minutes, the device vibrates. The idea of random reminders is interesting. One drawback is that it does not enable group synchronicity, but you could keep your watch and use them both.

Chapter 6: When You Have Problems

Problem #1: Where's the Beep?

Some of you will have problems with this system. What will happen to some of you is that you will stop hearing the beep. Don't be alarmed (pun intended). It's not uncommon for us to become accustomed to the sound and to tune it out. The prescription is pretty simple. Select an hour where you can afford to kill a minute, maybe 8:00 AM, maybe noon. Set your programmable alarm (the one you use for appointments or to wake up) for a minute before the hour and wait for the beep. That's it. By setting the alarm, you give yourself the opportunity to be attentive and SUCCEED in hearing the chime. You create a positive track record and in almost all cases your "disbeepaphobia" will pass.

Alternately, you might want to experiment with a different watch. Some digital watches emit a single beep when they chime and some emit a double beep. The double beep is much easier to recognize and may be the answer to your problem. You could experiment with a cooking timer if you just can't find a loud enough watch.

Problem #2: To Beep or Not to Beep, that is the Problem

People start growling at you when you beep inappropriately. Lets face it, generally church, meditation class, job interviews and your bedroom after midnight are all places in which you have no business beeping. You must become skilled in turning on and off your chime (the alternative is to take it off and stuff it into a thick pocket, purse or drawer). Return to Chapter 2: Mano a Mano with the Beeper, and practice. Turning the chime on and off is simply a matter of pressing the same two buttons sequentially. You can do it. And it affords a real smile when you get to turn it back on again because you know your going to feel great.

Beepalog I

Ultimately, your watch becomes part of a method involving a blend of new technology, integral simplicity and some repeating thoughts. Is this the best possible way to improve oneself? It really doesn't matter. What does matter is doing something. If you have means of effecting self-change that work for you; keep doing them, by all means. Try some of the ideas in this book. If they work for you, keep doing them until they stop working for you. It's not necessary to keep doing what doesn't work. What's most important is to utilize some method to systematically solve problems.

In the fifties, the Arthur D. Little Foundation engaged in some research on a group's abilities to solve problems. They observed that over 90% of groups that were not trained with a "methodology" failed to effectively solve problems. I suggest the reason so many people who use their watches as reminders do well is that it creates for them the foundation for a methodology. The chime reminds them to activate the method or process.

Consider the meaning of the term "thoughtful." Being thoughtful means being able to regularly consider another person's condition and respond in a caring manner. Digital chiming is a method that requires repetitive recall and thus the beep becomes a powerful primary mechanism for becoming more thoughtful. How many of us could use occasional improvement in our level of thoughtfulness?

Your watch could be the metronome for the music of your transformation.

This watch thing is contagious. It will start you grinning. And if you succeed in getting others to beep with you, the fun will really commence. When you start beeping together someone will always verbally comment. And once it catches on, you'll applaud, hoot, cheer or just giggle.

Years ago, I visited a "Moonie" indoctrination center in Northern California to find a young woman for whom some friends were concerned. I discovered that they had mastered the art of using little ritualistic "cheers" that boosted group energy. Everyone was empowered to call for a group cheer, and the group always responded. Despite the clear drawbacks in cult membership, I recognized that group reminders could create a powerful sense of belonging and boost group energy. My energy goes up even when I'm miles away from my beeping friends. I know they just thought of me … just as I thought of them. These few affectionate thoughts create a little rush … and a lot of them can make for a great day.

Beepalog II

It's important for me to dedicate a portion of this book to the spiritual aspect of mindfulness. One of my concerns in moving in this direction is my fear of invalidating the scientific arguments speaking to the health benefits of directed attention. Often the word "spiritual" conjures up for many the fear of having to accept something based solely on faith. And I agree that sometimes the word "spiritual" is used to bolster weak argument and false logic.

So let me define what spiritual means for me. Spiritual is that which makes me feel connected to something bigger, something greater than the sum of the parts. I believe that the most powerful use of reminders is to create connection. If I could, I'd plant a seed, a reminder that would have a significant portion of the people on this planet stopping on the hour, every hour, to consider their connectedness, perhaps even to look around and see who's with them at that moment.

Let me be so daring as to suggest again that the most powerful way to transform this planet is to establish a new custom of hourly consideration. One thing that happens at the same moment all over the planet is when the minute hand reaches 12 (:00 for digital). It is our opportunity to create synchronicity of the most ordinary and yet the most powerful kind. A new custom of kindness could replace the disappearing spiritual practices of a secular world.

Imagine if we all set to our watches to chime at exactly the same moment all over the planet. Imagine if we all agreed at that moment to come to a positive awareness and to connect with goodwill to those around us. It could almost be as powerful as the invention of the concept of "thank-you." Beep and look up to see who might be looking back at you.

Here's looking at you!

If you like this idea, start setting your watch to the National Observatory at 900/410-TIME, and spread the idea via e-mail or conversation that all of us respond to our hourly beeps by pausing to connect to those around us in addition to what else we may want to consider.

Afterward

I'm sitting on a houseboat on the Skagit River in Washington state with a visiting cat, Jake, and listening to the moving water behind the sounds of National Public Radio's evening news program, *All Things Considered.*

I'm enjoying letting my mind wander, transforming the experience of writing. I remember reading a book, *Writing Down the Bones,* that said just to write something every day.

Once attained, every new ability seems less deserving the awe once accorded. By the time I started paying my bills on time it didn't seem so hard. I'm waiting for that to happen on the guitar. Languages are like that too. I've little awe for people who speak Chinese, because I do. I do, however, stand in awe of people who speak languages I don't.

What I love about this watch thing is that it seems so easy and natural that I don't make a big thing about it. It's a piece of human attainment that, once achieved, cannot be taken away. Having read this, try hearing a watch beep and NOT think something … it's virtually impossible. It's like trying to remember to forget something.

I used to have awe for those with disciplined minds capable of great thoughtfulness. But now I, too, have developed that ability, with a little help from a beep.

The next level of integration comes when one's mindfulness is no longer beep-dependent. A parent is no longer running behind you holding onto the bicycle, you're riding on your own. Only you don't know, you think they're still there, so you keep going on your own. Your mind is growing up. Zoom!

Appendix

Following, you will find SOME instructions that will work with SOME models of SOME of the more popular digital watch brands. These instructions will work for SOME watches even if the watch in the illustration does not exactly match your watch. If you find that the directions don't work for your watch and you don't want to buy a new watch just to get the manufacturer's instructions, you may be able to reach the manufacturer and either find the instructions on the Internet or petition the manufacturer to send you a new set. Here are three of the biggest manufacturers:

- Timex can be reached at www.timex.com
- Casio can be reached at 1-800/YO-CASIO
- Armitron can be reached at 1-718/482-4195

Instructions for some Timex watches were included in Chapter 2 and following are instructions for some Casio, and Armitron watches.

Instructions for some models of Casio watches

Setting the time

Look at the following diagram (because, if you're like many of us, you'll need a magnifying glass to read the watch face itself).

Chime display

The watch has four buttons. Just to keep this simple, we'll call them 1, 2, 3 and four. We'll start by setting your watch for noon on January 1 — New Years Day.

1. Press Button #1 once to enter time-setting mode.

2. Press Button #3 once and the seconds go to "00".

3. Press button #2 to set the hours flashing. Press button #3 to advance the hour once per press, or hold it down to set the hours streaming.

4. Press button #2 again to flash the minutes. Press button #3 to advance the minutes.

5. Press button #2 again to advance month, then date and then day of week. And press button #3 to advance each in turn.

6. Press button #1 to end the setting process.

That wasn't so hard. Let's repeat that process. Start with step #1 and set your watch for Christmas morning — 6:00 AM on December 25.

1. Press Button #1 until the seconds flash.

2. Press Button #3 to zero out the seconds.

3. Press button #2 to set the hours flashing. Press button #3 to advance the hour.

4. Press button #2 again to flash the minutes. Press button #3 to advance them.

5. Press button #2 again to advance month, then date and then day of week. And press button #3 to advance each in turn.

6. Press button #1 to end the setting process.

Fantastic! Now, set your watch for the fireworks — 9:00 PM on Sunday, July 4.

1. Press Button #1 until the seconds flash.

2. Press Button #3 to zero out the seconds.

3. Press button #2 to set the hours flashing. Press button #3 to advance the hour.

4. Press button #2 again to flash the minutes. Press button #3 to advance them.

5. Press button #2 again to advance month, then date and then day of week. And press button #3 to advance each in turn.

6. Press button #1 to end the setting process.

One more drill and we'll do the 900 number. Set your watch for Day Light Savings Time — 2:00 AM on Saturday, April 15.

1. Press Button #1 until the seconds flash.

2. Press Button #3 to zero out the seconds.

3. Press button #2 to set the hours flashing. Press button #3 to advance the hour.

4. Press button #2 again to flash the minutes. Press button #3 to advance them.

5. Press button #2 again to advance month, then date and then day of week. And press button #3 to advance each in turn.

6. Press button #1 to end the setting process.

All right! Now, get ready. This call will cost 50¢. When you dial 900-410-TIME, you'll hear a man reading the time in 5- and 10- second intervals. (What a boring job.) He'll say something like, "US Naval Observatory Master Clock. At the tone Eastern Daylight Time 16 hours, 45 minutes and 50 seconds. US Naval Observatory Master Clock. At the tone Eastern Daylight Time 16 hours, 45 minutes and 55 seconds." Remember, your watch's seconds zero out when you press button #1, so you will be waiting like a puma ready to pounce, when this joker says, "US Naval Observatory Master Clock. At the tone Eastern Daylight Time 16 hours, 46 minutes exactly." So, get your watch ready; cradle the phone and dial 900-410-TIME.

1. Press Button #1 until the seconds flash.

2. Press Button #3 to zero out the seconds when he says the word "exactly."

3. Press button #2 to set the hours flashing. Press button #3 to advance the hour. Remember that he is reading the time for Eastern Daylight time; you will need to take this into consideration.

4. Press button #2 again to flash the minutes. Press button #3 to advance them.

5. Press button #2 again to advance month, then date and then day of week. And, of course, press button #3 to advance each in turn. The guy from the observatory won't help with these items.

6. Press button #1 to end the setting process.

Congratulations! You can now travel from time zone to time zone, fall back in the Fall and spring forward in the Spring. And you're precisely synchronized. All that remains is the matter of learning to turn the chime off and on. This is so easy!

Casio Chime On, Casio Chime Off

To set the chime on and off you only need to use buttons #2 and #4. Check out the diagram. See the little circle? That is where the little symbol for the chime will appear. If you look at your watch and see nothing, that is because the chime is not turned on. Here's how it works:

- Press button #2 once. You'll notice the letters "AL" in the upper left-hand corner of the screen.

-

- Press button #4 once. Then again. Then again. Then again. You'll notice the watch cycles through displaying two symbols. The upper one — little tick marks — indicates the chime. The lower one — a bell — represents the alarm. For our purposes, we only care about the chime.

-

- Press button #2 again to end the process.

So, let's try this. Press button #2 to bring up the "AL" screen. Press button #4 until you are sure the chime and alarm are turned off (neither symbol is visible). Press Button #2 once to end the process. You've just turned off the chime and are ready for church, bed or the cinema.

You awake in the morning. You're ready to begin your day's beeping. You grab your watch (come on, let's do this, now) press button #2, press button #4 until you see just the symbol for the chime, press button #2 once.

Time to go to the movies? Press button #2, Button #4 until no symbols for chime/alarm are visible, and button #2 once. That's it, dude. Done. You're trained. Ready to take your responsible place in beeping society. I'm proud of you. Your pew-sitting neighbors are proud of you and admit it, you're proud of yourself. Right?

Instructions for some models of Armitron watches

Setting the time

Look at the following diagram (because, if you're like many of us, you'll need a magnifying glass to read the watch face itself).

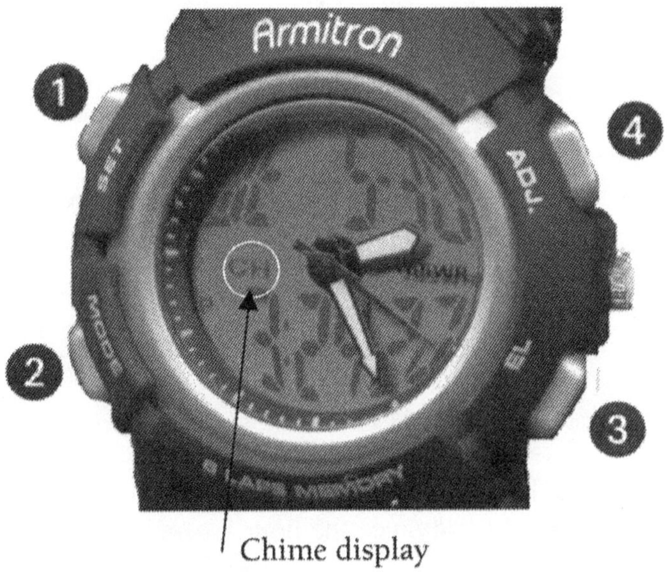

Chime display

The watch has four buttons. Just to keep this simple, we'll call them 1, 2, 3 and four. We'll start by setting your watch for noon on January 1 — New Years Day.

1. Press Button #1 once to enter time-setting mode.

2. Press Button #4 once and the seconds go to "00".

3. Press button #2 to set the hours flashing. Press button #4 to advance the hour once per press, or hold it down to set the hours streaming.

4. Press button #2 again to flash the minutes. Press button #4 to advance the minutes.

5. Press button #2 again to advance month, then date and then day of week. And press button #4 to advance each in turn.

6. Press button #1 to end the setting process.

That wasn't so hard. Let's repeat that process. Start with step #1 and set your watch for Christmas morning — 6:00 AM on December 25.

6. Press Button #1 until the seconds flash.

7. Press Button #4 to zero out the seconds.

8. Press button #2 to set the hours flashing. Press button #4 to advance the hour.

9. Press button #2 again to flash the minutes. Press button #4 to advance them.

10. Press button #2 again to advance month, then date and then day of week. And press button #4 to advance each in turn.

11. Press button #1 to end the setting process.

Fantastic! Now, set your watch for the fireworks — 9:00 PM on Sunday, July 4.

1. Press Button #1 until the seconds flash.

2. Press Button #4 to zero out the seconds.

3. Press button #2 to set the hours flashing. Press button #4 to advance the hour.

4. Press button #2 again to flash the minutes. Press button #4 to advance them.

5. Press button #2 again to advance month, then date and then day of week. And press button #4 to advance each in turn.

6. Press button #1 to end the setting process.

One more drill and we'll do the 900 number. Set your watch for Day Light Savings Time — 2:00 AM on Saturday, April 15.

1. Press Button #1 until the seconds flash.

2. Press Button #4 to zero out the seconds.

3. Press button #2 to set the hours flashing. Press button #4 to advance the hour.

4. Press button #2 again to flash the minutes. Press button #4 to advance them.

5. Press button #2 again to advance month, then date and then day of week. And press button #4 to advance each in turn.

6. Press button #1 to end the setting process.

All right! Now, get ready. This call will cost 50¢. When you dial 900-410-TIME, you'll hear a man reading the time in 5- and 10- second intervals. (What a boring job.) He'll say something like, "US Naval Observatory Master Clock. At the tone Eastern Daylight Time 16 hours, 45 minutes and 50 seconds. US Naval Observatory Master Clock. At the tone Eastern Daylight Time 16 hours, 45 minutes and 55 seconds." Remember, your watch's seconds zero out when you press button #1, so you will be waiting like a puma ready to pounce, when this joker says, "US Naval Observatory Master Clock. At the tone Eastern Daylight Time 16 hours, 46 minutes exactly." So, get your watch ready; cradle the phone and dial 900-410-TIME.

1. Press Button #1 until the seconds flash.

2. Press Button #4 to zero out the seconds when he says the word "exactly."

3. Press button #2 to set the hours flashing. Press button #4 to advance the hour. Remember that he is reading the time for Eastern Daylight time; you will need to take this into consideration.

4. Press button #2 again to flash the minutes. Press button #4 to advance them.

5. Press button #2 again to advance month, then date and then day of week. And, of course, press button #4 to advance each in turn. The guy from the observatory won't help with these items.

6. Press button #1 to end the setting process.

Congratulations! You can now travel from time zone to time zone, fall back in the Fall and spring forward in the Spring. And you're precisely synchronized. All that remains is the matter of learning to turn the chime off and on. This is so easy!

Armitron Chime On, Armitron Chime Off

To set the chime on and off you only need to use buttons #2 and #4. Check out the diagram. See the little circle? That is where the little symbol for the chime will appear — "CH". If you look at your watch and see nothing, that is because the chime is not turned on. Here's how it works:

- Press button #2 four times. You'll notice the letters "Al" in the upper left-hand corner of the screen.

- Press button #4 once. Then again. Then again. Then again. You'll notice the watch cycles through displaying two symbols. The "CH" — indicates the chime. The numeral "1" represents the alarm. For our purposes, we only care about the chime.

- Press button #2 again to end the process.

So, let's try this. Press button #2 four times to bring up the "Al" screen. Press button #4 until you are sure the chime and alarm are turned off (neither symbol is visible). Press Button #2 once to end the process. You've just turned off the chime and are ready for church, bed or the cinema.

You awake in the morning. You're ready to begin your day's beeping. You grab your watch (come on, let's do this, now) press button #2 four times, press button #4 until you see just the symbol for the chime, press button #2 once.

Time to go to the movies? Press button #2 four times, Button #4 until no symbols for chime/alarm are visible, and button #2 once. That's it, dude. Done. You're trained. Ready to take your responsible place in beeping society. I'm proud of you. Your pew-sitting neighbors are proud of you and admit it, you're proud of yourself. Right?

About the Author

Jim Lew is an independent consultant with a background in theater, education and psychotherapy. He has worked in diverse fields and has over two decades of experience facilitating groups, training, and consulting with organizations.

Jim has been self employed since 1982. Prior to that he was a teacher in the Chicago School System, a social worker for the State of Illinois, an employee with the Federal Office of Education as a trainer, system consultant, and presenter. Since becoming an independent, Jim has trained and consulted with the coal industry, Hollywood producers, corrections institutions, police departments, city governments, as well as Fortune 500 corporations.

Jim was raised in the Midwest and received his B.A. from Grinnell College in Iowa (1970), where he was student body president. His family had a Chinese restaurant on Route 66 in Amarillo as a child and later lived in Wichita until he left for Grinnell in 1966. Jim settled in Chicago in 1970 after meeting Saul Alinsky and becoming interested in community organizing.

After Mr. Alinsky died in 1971 Jim decided to become a psychotherapist. He trained in Transactional Analysis, Gestalt, and became certified in Neuro Linguistic Programming. In 1982 he transferred his group skills and learning models to the corporate sector. Mr. Lew has a twenty year relationship with members of the Lakota Tribe of Pine Ridge, S.D. Jim flies sailplanes, ultralights and gyrocopters.

Jim has trained, consulted, and been a presenter to numerous business and civic organizations ranging from the public sector to top corporations. Jim applies skills learned in therapeutic milieus to business situations to deal with difficult organizational problems. He has consulted with Bill and Hillary Clinton as well as the President of Hyatt Hotels. Jim has been training and presenting in the area of Diversity since the mid-eighties.

www.ingramcontent.com/pod-product-compliance
Lightning Source LLC
Chambersburg PA
CBHW031314060726

47590CB00003B/1205